# The Planets

Experts on reading levels
have consulted on the text and
concepts in this book.

At the end of the book is a "Look Back and Find" section
which provides additional information and encourages
the reader to refer back to previous pages
for the answers to the questions posed.

*Published by*
Franklin Watts, 96 Leonard Street, London EC2A 4RH

Franklin Watts Australia, 14 Mars Road, Lane Cove NSW 2066

ISBN: Paperback edition 0 7496 0516 2
Hardback edition 86313 192 1

© 1984 Franklin Watts/Aladdin Books

Paperback edition 1991

Hardback edition published
in the First Library series

*Designed and produced by:*
Aladdin Books Ltd, 28 Percy Street, London W1P 9FF

*Printed in Belgium*

# The Planets

by
Kate Petty

*Consultant*
Angela Grunsell

*Illustrated by*
Mike Saunders

Franklin Watts
London · New York · Toronto · Sydney

Did you know that you live on a planet
which is spinning round a star?
This star is called the Sun.
Your planet is called Earth.

Some planets have moons circling them.
Earth has one moon.
This is how our planet looks from space.

The planets look like stars but they are
quite different.
The stars are far-away suns which burn brightly.
Planets don't shine. They are lit up by the Sun.

The planets are much closer to us than the stars.
You can see them clearly with a small telescope.
You can even see some of Jupiter's moons.

The solar system is the name for the group of nine planets which go round the Sun.

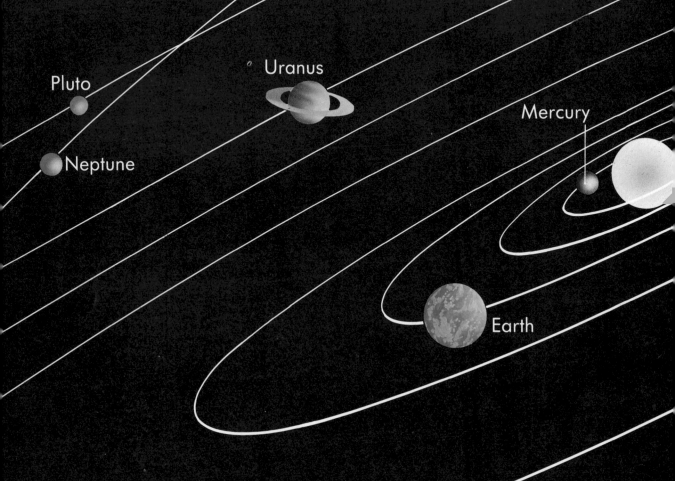

Pluto

Uranus

Mercury

Neptune

Earth

Each planet always follows its own path around the Sun. The path that planets travel is called an orbit.

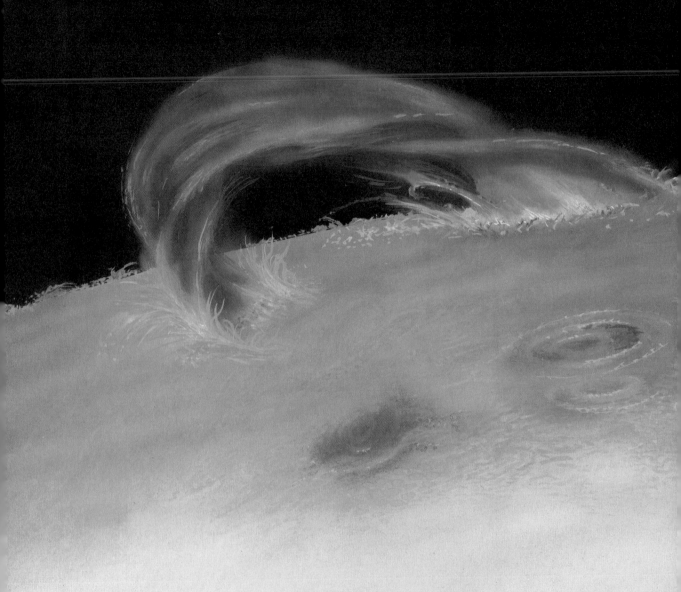

The Sun is more than a million times bigger
than Earth. Like other stars it is a
gigantic ball of flaming gases.

Even its surface, which is the coolest part,
bubbles and boils at a heat of 6000°C.
It shoots out flames
thousands of kilometres high.

All life on Earth depends on the Sun.
We also measure our time by it.
A year is the time it takes our planet
to go once round the Sun.

The planets spin like tops in their
orbits around the Sun.
Earth takes a day to spin around once.
Now we have begun to explore the other planets.

This rocket is blasting a space probe into space.
It is travelling to the planets.
There are no people on board.
The space probe carries cameras which can
send pictures back to Earth.

Mercury is the planet closest to the Sun.
It is unbearably hot there in the daytime.
Pictures taken by the space probe Mariner 10
show that Mercury looks very like our moon.

Venus looks like this.
Thick poisonous clouds blot out the Sun.
It is hot and always gloomy.
The air is so thick it would suffocate you.

No one could survive on Venus.
A space probe landed there and sent back
pictures to Earth. Just over an hour later
it was crushed and burned up.

Mars shines in the night sky with a reddish glow.
The rocky soil is a rusty red. Dust blown by
the wind makes the sky pink.

People used to think there might be life on Mars.
But so far, space probes have found nothing
living there at all.

Jupiter is the largest of all the planets.
It is made of swirling liquids and gases.
The 'red spot' is a huge storm.
Here it can be seen from one of its 16 moons.

Saturn's beautiful rings are formed from
billions of lumps of rock and ice.
Space probe Voyager 2 flew past these planets.
There were no solid surfaces to land on.

Uranus and Neptune are a long way from the Sun. They are dark and icy worlds. Voyager 2 should pass Uranus in 1986 and Neptune in 1989.

Far-away Pluto was not discovered until 1930.
Its strange orbit sometimes takes it closer
to the Sun than Neptune. From Pluto, the Sun
just looks like a bright star in the sky.

When you look up at the night sky it is strange
to think that people have landed on the moon
and space probes have visited the planets.
But the stars are other suns, far, far away.

Our Sun and the Solar System are only a speck
in our galaxy of stars.
There are millions of galaxies in the Universe.
No one knows where the Universe ends.

# Look back and find

What is our planet called?

How many moons does it have?

Why does our planet look blue?
*Because so much of the surface
is covered by water.*

Can you think of ways in which
we need the Sun?

Why do we have daylight and darkness?
*As the Earth spins, the side facing
the Sun has daylight while the other
is in darkness.*

Why could no one survive on Venus?

What makes Venus so hot?
*Venus is closer to the Sun
than Earth is. The thick air
on Venus traps the Sun's heat.*

How can you spot Mars at night?

Why did people once think
there might be life on Mars?
*Of all the planets Mars is the most like
Earth. It is not too hot or too cold
for there to be life. Scientists thought
there might be water there, too.*

How many moons does Jupiter have?

How big is Jupiter compared to Earth?
*Jupiter is 1300 times bigger than Earth.*

What is Saturn made of?
*It is made of liquids and gases, like Jupiter.*

Why are Uranus and Neptune so cold and icy?

How long will it take Voyager 2
to travel from Uranus to Neptune?

Why does the Sun look like a bright star
from Pluto?
*Because Pluto is so far away from the Sun.*

# Index